MEDITATION
IN ACTION

CHÖGYAM TRUNGPA

MEDITATION
IN ACTION

SHAMBHALA

Boston & London

1991

Shambhala Publications, Inc.
Horticultural Hall
300 Massachusetts Avenue
Boston, Massachusetts 02115
www.shambhala.com

12 11 10 9 8

Printed in Singapore

⊗ This edition is printed on acid-free paper that meets
the American National Standards Institute
Z39.48 Standard.
Distributed in the United States by Random House,
Inc., and in Canada by Random House of Canada Ltd

ISBN 0-87773-550-6   LC 90-533-5

The design on the cover is based on one of the seals
of the Trungpa Tulkus. It is the Sanskrit word *evam*
("thus"), which is used at the beginning of all sutras
("Thus have I heard"). At a deeper level, *e* represents
emptiness and *vam* the clear light.

CONTENTS

The Life and Example of
   Buddha   1

The Manure of Experience
   and the Field of Bodhi   25

Transmission   52

Generosity   62

Patience   85

Meditation   98

Wisdom   132

THE LIFE AND EXAMPLE OF BUDDHA

It is a clear, hot summer's day, and the thick branches of the sal trees are brilliant with flowers and heavy with their load of fruit. The landscape is wild and rocky with many caves, and the nearest town is more than a hundred miles away. In some of the caves are yogis with long matted hair, dressed only in a thin white cotton cloth. Some are sitting on deer skins and meditating. Others are performing various yogic practices, such as meditating while seated in the middle of a camp fire, which is a well-known ascetic practice. Yet others are reciting mantras or devotional chants. The place has an atmosphere of peace, solitude and stillness, but is also rather awesome. It might have remained unchanged since before the creation of the world. It is completely still and silent. There aren't even any birds singing. There is a great river nearby, but no fishermen. The river is so vast, it seems to be at least seven miles wide. On the bank ascetics are practicing the sacred ritual of purification. One sees them meditating and bathing in the river. That was the scene two thousand five hundred years ago in a certain place called Nairanjana in the province of Bihar in India.

A certain prince, called Siddhartha, arrives. His appearance is aristocratic; he has only recently removed his crown and his earrings and ornaments, so he feels rather naked. He has just sent away his horse and his last attendant, and now he puts on a clean white cotton cloth. He looks around him and tries to imitate the other ascetics. He wants to follow their example, so he approaches one of them and asks for instruction in the practice of meditation. First he explains that he is a prince and has found life in the palace to be meaningless. He has seen that there is birth, death, sickness and old age. He has also seen a sage walking along the street and this has inspired him. This is the example and the way of life he wants to follow. It is all new to him, and at first he cannot accept that this is actually happening. He cannot forget the luxuries and sensual enjoyments which he had in the palace and which are still revolving through his mind. This was prince Siddhartha, the future Buddha.

He then received instruction, perhaps rather unwillingly, from his present guru. He was given the ascetic practice of a rishi and taught to sit cross-legged and employ the seven postures of yoga and to practice yogic breathing exercises. At first it was so new to him that it was almost like a game. He also enjoyed the feeling of accomplish-

ment at having at last managed to leave his
worldly possessions to follow this wonderful way of life. The memory of his wife and
child and his parents was still very much
in his mind, which must have disturbed his
practice of yoga, but it seemed there was
no way to control the mind. And the yogis
never told him anything, except to follow
the ascetic practice.

This was Buddha's experience, then,
roughly two thousand five hundred years
ago. And one would find even now a very
similar landscape and have very similar experiences if one decided to leave home and
renounce hot and cold water baths and
forget about home cooking and the luxury
of riding in motor cars, or public transport
for that matter, which is still a great luxury. Some of us might go by airplane and
take only a few hours to get there: before
you know where you are, you are in the
middle of India. Some who are more ad-
venturous may, perhaps, decide to hitch-

hike. Nevertheless it would still seem un-real, the journey would be continually exciting and there would never be a dull moment. Finally we arrive in India. Per-haps in some ways it is disappointing. You will see a certain amount of moderniza-tion, and the snobbishness of the high-class, better-educated Indians, who are still imitating the British Raj. One might find it rather irritating at first, but some-how one accepts it and tries to leave the town as quickly as possible and head for the jungle. (In this case it may be a Tibetan monastery or an Indian ashram.) We could follow the same example and perhaps have more or less the same experience as prince Siddhartha. The first thing that would be very much on our minds would be the as-cetic aspect of it, or rather the absence of luxury. Now, would we learn anything from these first few days and months? Per-haps we would learn something of the way of life. But perhaps, because we had never seen such a country, we would be more inclined to be excited. One tends to interpret everything, and an internal conversation goes on in the mind as one struggles to break down the barriers of communication and language. One is still living very much in one's own world. Just as it was for Buddha, so for us the excitement and the novelty of being in a strange country would not wear out for several months. One would write letters home as if *possessed* by the country, intoxicated with excitement and the strangeness of it all. So if one returned after only a few days or weeks, one would not have learned very much, one would merely have seen a different country, a different way of life. And the same thing would have happened to Buddha if he had left the jungle of Nairanjana and returned to his kingdom in Rajgir.

In the case of Buddha, he practiced meditation for a long time under Hindu teachers, and he discovered that asceticism and merely conforming to one religious set up did not particularly help. He still didn't get the answer. Well, perhaps he got some answers. In a sense these questions were already answered in his mind, but he was more or less seeing what he wanted to see, rather than seeing things as they were. So in order to follow the spiritual path one must first overcome the initial excitement; that is one of the first essentials. For unless one is able to overcome this excitement, one will not be able to learn, because any form of emotional excitement has a blinding effect. One fails to see life as it is because one tends so much to build up one's own version of it. Therefore one should never commit oneself or conform to any religious or political structure without first finding the real essence of what one is looking for. Labeling oneself, adopting an ascetic way of life or changing one's costume—none of these brings about any real transformation.

After several years Buddha decided to leave. He had learned a great deal in a sense, but the time had come for him to say goodbye to his teachers, the Indian rishis, and to go off on his own. He went to a place quite a long way from there, although still on the bank of the Nairanjana river, and sat down under a pipal tree (which is also known as the Bodhi tree). For several long years he remained there, seated on a large stone, eating and drinking very little. This was not because he felt it necessary to follow the practice of strict asceticism, but he did feel it was necessary to remain alone and find things out for himself, rather than to follow someone else's example. He might have reached the same conclusions by different methods, but that is not the point. The point is that whatever one is trying to learn, it is necessary to have firsthand experience, rather than learning from books or from teachers or by merely conforming to an already established pattern. That is what he found, and in that sense Buddha was a great revolutionary in his way of thinking. He even denied the existence of Brahma, or God, the Creator of the world. He determined to accept nothing which he had not first discovered for himself. This does not mean to say that he disregarded the great and ancient tradition of India. He respected it very much. His was not an anarchistic attitude in any negative sense, nor was it revolutionary in the way the Communists are. His was real, positive revolution. He developed the creative side of revolution, which is not trying to get help from anyone else, but finding out for oneself. Buddhism is perhaps, the only religion which is not based on the revelation of God nor on faith and devotion to God or gods of any kind. This does not mean that Buddha was an atheist or a heretic. He never argued theological or philosophical doctrines at all. He went straight to the heart of the matter, namely how to see the truth. He never wasted time in vain speculation.

By developing such a revolutionary attitude one learns a great deal. For example, suppose one misses lunch one day. One may not be hungry, one may have had a large breakfast, but the *idea* of missing lunch affects one. Certain patterns are formed within the framework of society and one tends to accept them without questioning. Are we really hungry, or do we just want to fill up that particular midday time? That is a very simple and straightforward example. But much the same applies when we come to the question of ego.

Buddha discovered that there is no such thing as "I," ego. Perhaps one should say there is no such thing as "am," "I am." He discovered that all these concepts, ideas, hopes, fears, emotions, conclusions, are created out of one's speculative thoughts and one's psychological inheritance from parents and upbringing and so on. We just tend to put them all together, which is of course partly due to lack of skill in our educational system. We are told what to think, rather than to do real research from within ourselves. So in that sense asceticism, meaning the experience of bodily pain, is by no means an essential part of Buddhism. What is important is to get beyond the pattern of mental concepts which we have formed. That does not mean that we have to create a new pattern or try to be particularly unconventional and always go without lunch or what have you. We do not have to turn everything upside down in our pattern of behavior and in the way we present ourselves to other people. That again would not particularly solve the problem. The only way to solve the problem is by examining it thoroughly. From this point of view we have a certain desire—or not even as strong as desire—more a feeling of wanting to conform to something. And one does not even think about it, one is just led to it. So it is necessary to introduce the idea of *mindfulness*. Then we can examine ourselves each time, and go beyond mere opinions and so-called common sense conclusions. One must learn to be a skillful scientist and not accept anything at all. Everything must be seen through one's own microscope and one has to reach one's own conclusions in one's own way. Until we do that, there is no savior, no guru, no blessings and no guidance which could be of any help.

Of course, there is always this dilemma: if there is no help, then what are we? Are we nothing? Are we not trying to reach something higher? What is this higher thing? What, for example, is Buddhahood? What is enlightenment? Are they just nothing, or are they something? Well, I am afraid I am really no authority to answer this. I am merely one of the travelers, like everyone else here. But from my own experience—and my knowledge is, as the scripture describes it, "like a single grain of sand in the Ganges"—I would say that when we talk of "higher" things we tend to think in terms of our own point of view, a bigger version of ourselves. When we speak of God, we tend to think in terms of our own image, only greater, colossal, a kind of expansion of ourselves. It is like looking at ourselves in a magnifying mirror. We still think in terms of duality. I am here, He is there. And the only way to communicate is by trying to ask His help. We may feel we are making contact at certain times, but somehow we can never really communicate in this way. We can never achieve union with God, because there is a fixed concept, a prefabricated conclusion, which we have already accepted and we are merely trying to put that great thing into a small container. One cannot drive a camel through the eye of a needle. So we have to find some other means. And the only way to find it is to come back to the sheer simplicity of examining ourselves. This is not a question of trying to be "religious" or of making sure that one is kind to one's neighbor, or of giving as much money as possible to charity. Though of course these things may also be very good. The main point is that we should not merely accept everything blindly and try to fit it into the right pigeonhole, but try to see it at first hand from our own experience.

This brings us to the practice of meditation, which is very important. The trouble here is that one usually finds that books, teachings, lectures and so on are more concerned with proving that they are right than with showing *how* it is to be done, which is the essential thing. We are not particularly interested in spreading the teachings, but we are interested in making use of them and putting them into effect. The world is moving so fast, there is no time to *prove,* but whatever we learn, we must bring it and cook it and eat it immediately. So the whole point is that we must see with our own eyes and not accept any laid-down tradition as if it had some magical power in it. There is nothing magical which can transform us just like that. Although, being mechanically minded, we always look for something which will work by merely pressing a button. There is a great attraction in the short cut, and if there is some profound method which offers a quick way, we would rather follow that than undertake arduous journeys and difficult practices. So here we see the true importance of asceticism: punishing oneself leads nowhere, but some manual work and physical effort is necessary. If we go somewhere on foot, we know the way perfectly, whereas if we go by motor car or airplane we are hardly there at all, it becomes merely a dream. Similarly, in order to see the continual pattern of development, we have to go through it manually. That is one of the most important things of all. And here discipline becomes necessary. We have to discipline ourselves. Whether in the practice of meditation or in everyday life, there is a tendency to be impatient. On beginning something one tends to just taste it and then leave it; one never has the time to eat it and digest it properly and see the aftereffect of it. Of course, one has to taste for oneself and find out if the thing is genuine or helpful, but before discarding it one has to go a little bit further, so that at least one gets firsthand experience of the preliminary stage. This is absolutely necessary.

That is also what Buddha found. And that is why he sat and meditated on the bank of the Nairanjana for several years, hardly moving from the spot. He meditated in his own way, and he found that returning to the world was the only answer. When he discovered the awakened state of mind, he realized that leading an ascetic life and punishing oneself did not help, so he got up and went to beg for some food. The first person he met, near Bodhgaya, was a wealthy woman who owned many cows. She gave him some boiled condensed milk with honey in it, and he drank it and found it delicious. Not only that, but he found it greatly enhanced his health and energy, as a result of which he was able to make great progress in the practice of meditation. The same thing happened in the case of the great Tibetan yogi Milarepa. The first time he went out and received a properly cooked meal, he found that it gave him new strength and he was able to meditate properly.

Buddha then looked around for somewhere comfortable to sit, having decided that sitting on a stone seat was too hard and painful. A farmer gave him a bunch of kusa grass, and Buddha spread it under a tree at Bodhgaya and sat down there. He had discovered that trying to achieve something by force was not the answer, and in fact for the first time he accepted that there was nothing to achieve. He completely abandoned all ambition. He had his drink and he had his seat, and he made himself as comfortable as possible. That very night he finally attained sambodhi, the fully awakened state. But that wasn't quite enough, he hadn't quite overcome everything. All his hidden fears and temptations and desires, the last lash of ego, came to him in the form of Mara, the Evil One. First Mara sent his beautiful daughters to seduce him, but without success. Then came the fierce troops of Mara, the last tactic of the ego. But Buddha had already achieved the state of maitri, loving-kindness. In other words he was not just compassionate in the sense of looking down on Mara as stupid—for Mara was his own projection—but he had achieved the nonresisting state, the state of nonviolence, where he identified himself with Mara. In the scriptures it says that each arrow of Mara became a rain of flowers falling down on him. So finally the ego surrendered and he achieved the awakened state of mind. We ourselves might have such an experience, perhaps in a short glimpse of clarity and peace—the open state of mind—but that is not quite enough. We have to learn how to put that into effect, we have to use that as a kind of center from which we can expand. One has to create the situation around one, so that one does not have to say, "I am the awakened person." If one had to say such a thing and demonstrate it verbally, one would not be awakened.

Buddha then walked for about seven weeks. In a sense he was just alone, and one might say he was a very lonely person, as he was the only one who saw and who had achieved something. He knew some of the answers for dealing with life and for finding the true meaning, or *suchness,* in the world of samsara. But he was not quite sure how to present this and he almost decided not to speak. There is a gatha, or short verse, in one of the sutras where he says, "Profound peace without limit, such is the teaching I have found. But no one would be able to understand this, therefore I shall remain silent in the jungle." But then the true and final establishment of compassion came and he saw his ability to create the right situation. Up to this point he still had the desire to teach (because he had achieved something he felt that he should save the world — if one may use such an expression). But he had to give up this idea of saving all sentient beings. Then at the very moment when he had decided to leave the world and return to the jungle, the real, selfless compassion arose in him. He was no longer aware of himself as a teacher, he no longer had the idea that he had to save people, but whenever the situation presented itself he dealt with it spontaneously.

He preached and taught for about forty years, and spent his life walking from one end of India to the other. He did not ride on an elephant or a horse or a chariot, but simply walked barefoot all over India. I think if any of us had seen him or heard him talk, it would not have been anything like a lecture as we know it. It was just simple conversation. It was not the talking that was important but the whole situation that he created; it was not because he had achieved such spiritual power and thereby dominated the whole scene, but because he was simply being true—just as any of us could be. Therefore the teaching had been taught before he opened his mouth. That is why we find in the sutras that gods and *asuras* and all kinds of people from different parts of India attended his talks and saw him and met him, and all could understand him. They did not have to ask him questions, but they automatically received the answers. This is a wonderful example of communication. Buddha never claimed that he was an incarnation of God, or any kind of divine being. He was just a simple human being who had gone through certain things and had achieved the awakened state of mind. It is possible, partially possible at least, for any of us to have such an experience.

From this example we see that speech alone is not the only method of communication. There is already communication before we say anything, even if we are only saying "Hello," or "How are you?" Somehow communication also continues after we finish speaking. The whole thing must be conducted in a very skillful way, by being true and not self-centered. Then the concept of duality is absent and the right pattern of communication is established. It is only through one's own experience of searching that this can be achieved, and not through merely copying someone else's example. Neither asceticism nor any preconceived pattern will provide the answer. We have to make the first move ourselves rather than expecting it to come from the phenomenal world or from other people. If we are meditating at home and we happen to live in the middle of the High Street, we cannot stop the traffic just because we want peace and quiet. But we can stop ourselves, we can accept the noise. The noise also contains silence. We must put ourselves into it and expect nothing from outside, just as Buddha did. And we must accept whatever situation arises. As long as we never retreat from the situation, it will always present itself as a vehicle and we will be able to make use of it. As it is said in the scriptures, "The Dharma is good at the beginning, the Dharma is good in the middle and the

Dharma is good at the end." In other words the Dharma never becomes out of date, since fundamentally the situation is always the same.

THE MANURE OF EXPERIENCE AND THE FIELD OF BODHI

How to give birth to bodhi, the awakened state of mind? There is always great uncertainty when you don't know how to begin and you seem to be perpetually caught up in the stream of life. A constant pressure of thoughts, of wandering thoughts and confusion and all kinds of desires, continually arises. If you speak in terms of the man in the street, he doesn't seem to have a chance, because he is never really able to look inward; unless perhaps he reads some book on the subject and has the desire to enter into a disciplined way of life, and even then there seems to be no chance, no way to begin. People tend to make a very sharp distinction between spiritual life and everyday life. They will label a man as "worldly" or "spiritual," and they generally make a hard and fast division between the two. So if one speaks about meditation, awareness and understanding, then the ordinary person, who has never heard of such things, obviously would not have a clue and he probably would not even be sufficiently interested to listen properly. And because of this division he finds it almost impossible to take the next step and he can never really communicate with himself or with others in this particular way. The teachings, the instructions, the mystical writings, may all be very profound, but somehow he is never able to penetrate through to them, so he comes to a kind of dead end. Either a man is "spiritually inclined" or else he is a "worldly person," and there seems to be no way to bridge this gap. I think this is one of the great hindrances to the birth of bodhi. It also happens that people who have started on the path have doubts and want to give it up. They may perhaps think that they would be happier if they gave it up and just remained agnostics.

So there is something not quite flowing, there is a failure to relate one thing to another, and this is what prevents us from giving birth to bodhi. Therefore we have to study this problem. We have to provide some clue for the man in the street, some way of finding out, some concept that he can understand and which will still be related to his life and will still be part of his life. Of course, there is no magic word or miraculous thing which could suddenly change his mind. One wishes it were possible, by saying only a few words, to enlighten someone, but even great teachers like Christ or Buddha were unable to perform such a miracle. They had always to find the right opportunity and create the right situation. If one examines the character of the person and one studies the blockage, the difficulties, then one simply goes further and further, because one is trying to untie a knot which is already there, and it would take ages and ages to unravel this entanglement and confusion. So one has to approach from another angle and start off by just accepting the character of that person, who may be completely worldly minded, and then choose one particular aspect of his activity or mentality and use it as a ladder, as an anchor, as a vehicle, so that even the man in the street could give birth to bodhi. It is all very well to say that Buddha was an awakened person and that he is continuously living as far as the essence of the Buddha and his teachings are concerned—the universal law permeates everything, and to talk of the sangha, the highest and most open community which can influence things.

But still the majority of people could never even think of taking refuge along those lines. So somehow one has to find the right approach. And one always finds that a person has within himself a specific character. He may be regarded as having no intelligence and no personality at all, but each person in fact has his own particular quality. It may be a great kind of violence, or great laziness, but one has just to take that particular quality and not regard it necessarily as a fault or blockage, for that *is* the bodhi which is in him; it is the seed, or rather the full potentiality for giving birth—he is already impregnated by bodhi. As one particular scripture says, "Since Buddha-nature pervades all beings there is no such thing as an unsuitable candidate."

This scripture was composed after the death of Buddha, after the Parinirvana. In the world of gods and men everyone began to doubt whether the teachings of Buddha would remain, because it seemed that now the wonderful teacher was gone and all that remained was a group of mendicant monks, and they did not seem to do very much, or they were not able to do so. So one of the disciples was lamenting and saying that now the world of samsara will go on and on, with its waves of passion, desire, hatred and delusion; we will never have the chance to hear the Buddha's teaching and instructions, we are again plunged into darkness. So what shall we do? And as he lamented the answers came to his mind, that Buddha had never died, that his teaching is always present and that the birth and death of Buddha is merely a concept, an idea. In fact, no one is excluded and all beings—anyone who possesses consciousness, anyone who possesses mind, or the unconscious mind—all are candidates for bodhisattvahood, anyone can become an awakened person.

In this sense there is no such thing as a

"secret doctrine" or a teaching which is only for the few. As far as the teaching is concerned it is always open; so open in fact, so ordinary and so simple, that it is contained within the character of that particular person. He may be habitually drunk, or habitually violent, but that character is his potentiality. And in order to help give birth to bodhi, one must first of all respect that person's character and open one's heart to that violence in him. Then one must go into him fully and respect him so that the energetic, the dynamic aspect of violence can be made to serve as the energy aspect of the spiritual life. In this way the first step is taken and the first link is made. Probably the person feels very bad, that he is doing something wrong, or that something is not quite right. He may feel that he has big difficulties, that he has a problem which he wants to solve. But he cannot solve it, and probably in his search for a solution he merely substitutes other activities for the ones he has renounced. Therefore it is through simple, direct and ordinary things in the person's mind and behavior that he arrives at the realization of the awakened state of mind.

Of course one cannot apply this in a general way. It is no use generalizing or trying to explain philosophical concepts to a man in his state. One has to study that particular moment of the person, that very moment of nowness. And there is always a kind of spark, a kind of gap. His character is not just one thing. There is active behavior, then passive, then active, continuously changing, and the first moment producing and giving birth to the next moment. So there is always a gap between these two periods, and one has to take that as the starting point. Probably one has to begin with some form of theory, because without respecting samsara, the world of confusion, one cannot possibly discover the awakened state of mind, or nirvana. For samsara is the entrance, samsara is the vehicle for nirvana. Therefore one should say that the violent character is good. It is a wonderful thing, it is something positive. And then he begins to realize this, though at first he may be perplexed and wonder what is good in it, but somehow, if he gets beyond the fascination part of it, he at least begins to feel good; and he begins to realize that he is not just a "sinner" but that there is something very positive in him. It is exactly the same thing when one practices meditation. A person may begin to detect his own weaknesses. It may be in a mild form, as a wandering mind or planning for one's future, but certain things begin to come, and it is as though one were sitting specially to think these things over rather than to practice meditation. Through this one discovers certain things, and this is very valuable, it provides a wonderful opportunity.

It is often mentioned in the scriptures that without theories, without concepts, one cannot even start. So start with concepts and then build up theory. And then you use up the theory and it gradually gives way to wisdom, to intuitive knowledge, and that knowledge finally links with reality. So to start with, one should allow and not react against things. And if one wants to help a person, for example, there are two ways of doing it: one is that you want to help him because you want him to be different, you would like to mold him according to your idea, you would like him to follow your way. That is still compassion with ego, compassion with an object, compassion finally with results which will benefit you as well—and that is not quite true compassion. This plan to help other people may be a very good one, but nevertheless the emotional approach of wanting to save the world and bring peace is not quite ꞌ ꞏgh; there has to be more than that, there has to be more depth. So first one has to start by respecting concepts and then build from there. Though actually in Buddhist teachings, concepts are generally regarded as a hindrance. But being a hindrance does not mean that it prevents anything. It is a hindrance and it is also the vehicle—it is everything. Therefore one must pay special attention to concepts.

It is said, I think in the *Lankavatara Sutra,* that unskilled farmers throw away their rubbish and buy manure from other farmers, but those who are skilled go on collecting their own rubbish, in spite of the bad smell and the unclean work, and when it is ready to be used they spread it on their land, and out of this they grow their crops. That is the skilled way. In exactly the same way, the Buddha says, those who are unskilled will divide clean from unclean and will try to throw away samsara and search for nirvana, but those who are skilled bodhisattvas will not throw away desire and the passions and so on, but will first gather them together. That is to say, one should first recognize and acknowledge them, and study them and bring them to realization. So the skilled bodhisattva will acknowledge and accept all these negative things. And this time he really knows that he has all these terrible things in him, and although it is very difficult and unhygienic, as it were, to work on, that is the only way to start. And then he will scatter them on the field of bodhi. Having studied all these concepts and negative things, when the time is right he does not keep them anymore, but scatters them and uses them as manure. So out of these unclean things comes the birth of the seed which is realization. This is how one has to give birth. And the very idea that concepts are bad, or such-and-such a thing is bad, divides the whole thing, with the result that you are not left with anything at all to deal with. And in that case you either have to be completely perfect, or else battle through all these things and try and knock them all out. But when you have this hostile attitude and try to suppress things, then each time you knock one thing out another springs up in its place, and when you attack that one, another one comes up from somewhere else. There is this continual trick of the ego, so that when you try to disentangle one part of the knot, you pull on the string and only make it tighter somewhere else, so you are continually trapped in it. Therefore the thing is not to battle any more, not to try and sort out the bad things and only achieve good, but respect them and acknowledge them. So theory and concepts are very good, like wonderful manure. Through thousands and thousands of lives we have been collecting so much rubbish that now we have a wonderful wealth of this manure. It has everything in it, so it would be just the right thing to use, and it would be such a shame to throw it away. Because if you do throw it away, then all your previous life until today, maybe twenty, thirty or forty years, will have been wasted. Not only that, but lives and lives and lives will have been wasted, so one would have a feeling of failure. All that struggle and all that collecting would have been wasted, and you would have to start all over again from the beginning. Therefore, there would be a great feeling of disappointment, and it would be more a defeat than anything having been gained. So one has to respect the continual pattern. One may have broken away from the origin and all sorts of things may have happened. These may not be particularly good things. They are rather undesirable and negative. At this stage there are good things and bad things, but this collection contains good things disguised as bad and bad things disguised as good.

One must respect the flowing pattern of all one's past lives and the early part of one's present life right up to today. And there is a wonderful pattern in it. There is already a very strong current where many streams meet in a valley. And this river is very good and contains this powerful current running through it, so instead of trying to block it one should join this current and use it. This does not mean that one should go on collecting these things over and over again. Whoever does that would be lacking in awareness and wisdom, he would not have understood the idea of collecting manure. He could collect it together and acknowledge it, and by acknowledging it he would have reached a certain point and would understand that this manure is ready to be used.

There is a story in the teachings of tantra about two close friends who both wanted to search for the truth. They went to a master, and the master said, "Do not abandon anything, accept everything. And once having accepted, use it in the right way." And the first one thought, "Well, this is wonderful. I can go on being just the way I am." So he set up hundreds of brothels and hundreds of butcher shops and hundreds of drinking places, which in India was regarded as something that only a lower-caste person would do. He began to run all these big businesses, and he thought this was what he was supposed to do. But the other friend thought this was not quite right and he began to examine himself; and by examining himself he came to the conclusion that he had enough material already and did not have to collect any more. He did not have to do any particular practice of meditation, but by acknowledging the already existing heap, he achieved enlightenment, or at least a certain stage of realization, a kind of satori. Then one day they met each other and talked together and compared their experiences. The first one was not at all awakened; he was still struggling and collecting and doing all these things. In fact he had fallen into an even worse trap and had not even started to examine himself. But each of them was quite sure that he was right, so they both decided to go and consult the teacher. And the teacher said "I am afraid your way is wrong" to the one who was running the businesses. And he was so disappointed that he drew his sword and murdered the teacher on the spot.

There are these two possible approaches, and there may perhaps be some confusion between the two. Nevertheless, if a person is skilled enough—not necessarily intelligent—but skilled enough and patient enough to sift through his rubbish and study it thoroughly, then he will be able to it. So, coming back to the subject of concepts, which is a very important example, the idea behind this is to develop a positive outlook and to recognize your great wealth. And having recognized one's concepts and ideas, one must also, in a sense, cultivate them. One has a tendency to try and abandon them or throw them away. But one should cultivate them, not in the sense of reading more books and having more discussions and philosophical disputes—that would be the other way, the way of the friend who ran the businesses—but simply, since you already have enough wealth, just go through it. Just as a person who wants to buy something first has to check and see how much money he has. Or else it is like going back to your old diaries and studying them, and seeing your different stages of development, or going up to the attic and opening up all the old boxes to find the old dolls and toys that were given to you when you were three years old, and looking at them and examining them together with their associations. In this way you gain a complete understanding of what you are, and that is more important than continuously creating. The point of realization is not to try and understand only the awakened state and pretend not to understand the other side, because that becomes a way of cheating oneself. You see, you are your own best friend, your own closest friend, you are the best company for yourself. One knows one's own weaknesses and inconsistency, one knows how much wrong one has done, one knows it all in detail, so it doesn't help to try and pretend you don't know it, or to try not to think of that side and only think of the good side; that would mean that one was still storing one's rubbish. And if you store it like that you would not have enough manure to raise a crop from this wonderful field of bodhi. So you should go through and study even right back to your childhood, and of course if you have the great ability to go back to your previous lives, you should do so and try to understand them.

There is also a story about Brahma, who came one day to hear the Buddha preach, and the Buddha asked, "Who are you?" And Brahma for the first time began to look and check into himself (Brahma personifying the ego), and when he first looked into himself he couldn't bear it. He said, "I'm Brahma, the Great Brahma, the Supreme Brahma." So Buddha asked, "Why do you come and listen to me?" And Brahma said, "I don't know." Buddha then said to him, "Now, look back into your past." So Brahma, with his wonderful ability to see his many past lives, looked; and he couldn't bear it. He simply broke down and wept in front of Buddha. Then Buddha said, "Well done, well done, Brahma! That is good." You see, this was the first time that Brahma had used his wonderful ability to see into his distant past, and so he finally saw things clearly. This does not mean that a person has to break down and feel bad about it, but it is very important to check and go through everything so that nothing is unexplored. Having started from there one gains a complete view of the whole thing—like an aerial view which takes in the whole landscape, all the trees and the road and everything—without there being anything that one pretends not to see.

One must also examine fear and expectation. If there is fear of death, one examines that; if one fears old age, one examines that. If one feels uneasy about a certain ugliness in oneself, or a certain disability or physical weakness of any kind, one examines them as well. And one should also examine one's mental image of oneself, and anything one may feel bad about. It is very painful in the beginning— as Brahma showed by breaking down— when you first go through it and see it. But this is the only way to do it. Sometimes one touches on a very painful spot where one is almost too shy to look into it, but somehow one still has to go through it. And by going into it one finally achieves a real command of oneself, one gains a thorough knowledge of oneself for the first time. Now, we have explored the negative aspects, and have also probably gained some idea of the positive side. We still have not attained anything, we have just started the basic collection of manure, and now we have to study it and see how to put it to use.

By now one has developed this positive outlook and one has achieved a certain amount of understanding, and that is what is known as real theory. It is still theory, but you do not throw it overboard. In fact you cultivate this kind of theory and you continuously work on and on intellectually; intellectualizing only up to a certain point, of course, but still working on and on—and without having reference to books or talks or discussions. It has to be a kind of contemplation and firsthand study. One's theory then begins to develop and takes on a shape of its own. And then you begin to discover not only the positive things you have done, but also the element of bodhi which is in you. You begin to realize that you have this great ability to create such a wonderful theory. At this stage, of course, a person often feels that he has reached a state of enlightenment, a state of satori, but this is a mistake. Naturally, at this first discovery, there is great excitement, great joy, bliss, but he still has to go on. So, having gone through these things, and having studied and explored them, one finds that one's theory does not stop, as ordinary theory does after reading books on philosophy—or scriptures, for that matter. But this theory continues. There is a continual investigation, a continual finding out. Sometimes of course this theory does stop. One reaches a certain point where one becomes too much fascinated by the whole thing; one searches with too much eagerness, and then one comes to a stop and can't go any further. That doesn't mean there is a breakdown or a blockage, it means one is trying too much with an idea, one is trying too much with the inquisitive mind. Then one has to channel it differently, without the eagerness and without the fascination, but going step by step—as it says in the scriptures: at an elephant's pace. You have to walk very slowly, unemotionally. But walk with dignity, step by step, like an elephant walking in the jungle.

So, your continual struggle may be a very slow one, but Milarepa says, "Hasten slowly and you will soon arrive." By this time theory is no longer theory. Well, it is also a kind of imagination. So many imaginary things come in. And this imagination may even be a kind of hallucination, but again, one does not abandon that. One does not regard it as a wrong track, as though one had to go back to the right one. In fact, one uses imagination. So theory brings imagination, which is the beginning of intuitive knowledge. One then discovers that one has a great imaginative energy, and so one goes on, gradually, step by step. In the next stage one goes beyond just imagination—and this is not hallucination at all. There is something in us which is more real than merely imagination, though it is still colored by imagination. It is somehow ornamented by this sort of imaginary outline, but at the same time there is something in it. It is like reading a children's book, for example; it is written for children and it is entirely imaginary, but there is something in it as well. Perhaps the writer simplifies his experience, or tries to be childlike, so one finds something in it. And the same is true of any story, for that matter. And that imagination is not just hallucination, but real imagination. If one looks back to theory, or if one traces back to the first steps one took, it may seem a bit tiring or even unnecessary, but it isn't so. One hasn't wasted time at all.

You have scattered the manure very evenly over the field and now is the time to sow the seed and wait for the crop to grow. That is the first preparation, and now one is ready to discover. And that discovery has already begun to develop. There are many questions one would like to ask and many things are still not certain. But in fact at that stage one doesn't really need to ask questions at all, perhaps one simply needs an external person to say that it is so, although the answer is already in one. The question is like the first layer, like the skin of an onion, and when you remove it the answer is there. This is what the great logician and philosopher of Buddhism, Asanga, described as "the intuitive mind." In the intuitive mind, if one studies true logic, one finds that the answers—and the opponent's attitude—are in us. So we

don't have to search for the answer, because the question contains the answer in
it. It is a matter of going into it in depth;
that is the true meaning of logic. At this
stage one has reached a kind of feeling; the
imagination becomes a kind of feeling.
And with that feeling it is as though one
has reached the entrance hall.

TRANSMISSION

So after all your preparation you are finally
ready to give birth to bodhi. And the next
thing you have to do is to go to a guru, a
teacher, and ask him to show you the
awakened state—as if he possessed your
wealth. It is as though someone else possesses your own belongings and you are
asking him to give them back to you. Well,
that is what it is in fact, but one has to go
through the kind of ritual of it. When you
have asked him, the teacher will instruct.
That is what is known as transmission. The
term *transmission* or *abhisheka* is used particularly in the Vajrayana teachings and the
teachings of Buddhist yoga. It is used a
great deal in the Tibetan tradition and also
in the Zen tradition. Transmission does not
mean that the teacher is imparting his
knowledge or his discovery to you—that

would be impossible; even Buddha could not do so. But the whole point is that we stop collecting any more things, and we just manage to empty out whatever we have. And to avoid collecting any more, to avoid charging up the ego, it is necessary to ask some external person to give something, so that you feel that something is given to you. Then you don't regard it as your wealth which he is giving back to you, but as something very precious of his. So one must also be very grateful to the teacher. And that is a great protection against the ego, since you do not look on it as something discovered within yourself, but as something which someone else has given you. He gives you this gift; although in reality the transmission is not, as we said, something given to you, it is simply discovered within oneself. All the teacher can do is to create the situation. He will create the right situation and because of this situation and environment the pupil's

mind will also be in the right state, because he is already there. It is like going to
the theater: things are already built up for
you—the seats and the stage and so on—
so even by the very fact of going into it
one feels automatically that one is taking
part in some particular event. Whenever
we go into a place or participate in something we become a part of it because the
environment is already created. In the case
of transmission the situation may be rather
different, but nevertheless, there is still a
certain environment. The teacher may not
use words at all, or perhaps he goes to
great lengths to explain the subject, or he
may perform a ceremony of some kind, or
else he may do something quite ridiculous.

There is the story of Naropa, the great
Indian pandit, the maha pandita, or great
pandit, in the University of Nalanda. He
was one of the four great pandits at that
particular period of Buddhist history; he
was known as *the* great pandit in India—

in the whole of the world for that matter.
He could recite all the sacred scriptures by
heart and he knew all the philosophy and
everything, but he was not satisfied with
himself because he was merely giving out
what he had learned, but he never really
learned the depths of it. So one day as he
was walking on the balcony of the university he heard a group of beggars talking by
the main entrance. He heard them saying
that there was a great yogi called Tilopa,
and when he heard this name he was quite
sure that this was the right guru for him,
so he decided to go in search of him. He
gave gifts of food to these people and asked
them where Tilopa lived. They told him
where to go. But even so it took him about
twelve months of searching. Each time he
thought he had found the right place he
was told to go somewhere else. And finally
he came to a little fishing village and he
asked for the great yogi Tilopa. One of the
fishermen said, "Well, I don't know about

a "great yogi," but there is a Tilopa who lives down by the river. He is very lazy and doesn't even fish, and he just lives on what 'the fishermen throw away—the heads and the entrails of the fish and all that." Naropa followed his directions. But when he came to the place all he saw was a beggar, a very mild-looking character, who appeared to be unable even to speak. However, he prostrated and asked him for teaching. For three days Tilopa said nothing, but finally he nodded his head. Naropa took that to mean that he accepted him as his disciple. Then Tilopa said, "Follow me," so he followed him for twelve long years and underwent many hardships and difficulties during that time. On one particular occasion Tilopa said he was very hungry. (I mention this because it is all part of transmission. You see, he was creating the right environment.) So he asked him to find some food. Now, Naropa was a very refined person—he was born in a

Brahmin family—but he had to lead this kind of life, following the example of Tilopa. So he went to a village where they were having a wedding feast, or a special feast of some kind, and first he tried to beg, but it was forbidden to beg on that particular feast day. He crept into the kitchen and stole a bowl of soup and ran away and gave it to his guru. Tilopa seemed very pleased. In fact it was the first time Naropa had ever seen such a wonderful smiling expression on his face. He thought, "Well, this is wonderful. I think I'll go and fetch a second bowl." Tilopa expressed his approval and said he would like another bowl. But this time they caught Naropa and beat him and broke all his legs and arms and left him lying on the ground, half dead. A few days later Tilopa came up and said, "Well, what's the matter with you? Why didn't you come back?" He seemed rather angry. So Naropa said, "I'm dying." But his guru said, "Get up! You're not dying, and you still have to follow me for several years yet." And he got up and felt all right, and in fact nothing was wrong.

On another occasion they came to a deep canal which was infested with leeches. Tilopa said he wanted to cross over and asked Naropa to lie down across the canal to act as a bridge. So he lay down in the water. And when Tilopa had walked over him, Naropa found that his body was covered with hundreds of leeches, and he was again left lying there for several days. Things like this happened all the time, until finally, in the last month of the twelfth year, Tilopa was sitting with him one day and suddenly took off his sandal and hit him in the face with it. At that very moment the teachings of mahamudra, which means "the great symbol," came like a flash into Naropa's mind and he attained realization. After that, there was a great feast, and Tilopa told him, "That is all I can show you. All my teachings have now been transmitted to you. In the future, if anyone wants to follow the path of maha-mudra, he must learn and receive instructions from Naropa. Naropa is like a second king after me." Only after that did Tilopa explain the teachings to him in detail.

So, that is one example of "transmission." Of course in those days people were more patient and could afford to spend such a long time and were also prepared to do so. But the idea is not that Naropa received the teaching only at the moment when the shoe hit his head; the process was going on all the time during those twelve long years that he spent with his teacher. All these difficulties and different stages that he went through were part of the transmission. It is a question of building up and creating the atmosphere. In the same way certain ceremonies of transmission, abhisheka ceremonies, are part of a process of creating an environment, which includes the room and the person and the very fact of saying, "In three days time I will instruct you, and the transmission will take place then." In this way the disciple will mentally open himself. And when he has opened himself the teacher will say a few words, which probably do not mean very much. Or perhaps he will not say anything. The important thing is to create the right situation both on the teacher's part and on the pupil's part. And when the right situation is created then suddenly the teacher and pupil are not there anymore. The teacher acts as one entrance and the pupil acts as another, and when both doors are open there is a complete emptiness, a complete oneness between the two. This is what is known in Zen terminology as "the meeting of two minds." When one has finally solved the last koan, both are silent. The Zen master wouldn't say, "You are right" or "Now you've got it." He stops. And the pupil just stops. And there is a moment of silence. That is transmission—

creating the right situation—that is as much as an external guru can do. It is also as much as you can do. Transmission is merely opening up on both sides, opening the whole thing. One opens oneself completely in such a way that, although it may only be for a few seconds, it somehow means a great deal. That doesn't mean one has reached enlightenment, but one has had a glimpse of what reality is. And this is not particularly exciting or startling, it is not necessarily a very moving experience. Something just opens, there is a kind of flash, and that's all. Although one sees it described in books as "great bliss" or "mahamudra" or "the awakened state of mind" or "satori"—all sorts of titles and names are given. But somehow the actual moment is very simple, very direct. It is merely a meeting of two minds. Two minds become one.

GENEROSITY

Generosity, dana, is one of the six paramitas, or transcendent actions. *Par* means literally "the other shore." In fact this is still used colloquially in India; *par* — meaning the other side of the river. *Mita* is one who got there. So *paramita* means that which has reached the other shore. Certain scholars refer to the paramitas as the six perfections. In one sense they are perfect actions, but the word *perfection* also has other connotations which are not pertinent. The aim is not to try and achieve perfection; therefore it is better to see the paramitas in terms of transcendence — as going beyond.

These six transcendent actions are the actions of the bodhisattva. *Bodhi* means the awakened state of mind, and *sattva* is the person who is on the way to the awakened state. So the word *bodhisattva* refers to those who have achieved and those who have an inclination to follow the path of compassion, the path of love. The Hinayana path, the "Lesser Vehicle"—known as the elementary path or the narrow path—is based on discipline, the first requirement for the development of freedom. And this path disciplines not only mind, through the practice of meditation but also speech and physical behavior. Discipline of this sort is quite different from laying down a moral code of law or moralizing in the sense of "sin" and "virtue"; it concerns acting properly, acting truly, acting thoroughly, acting according to the law of what is. So we must see this concept of discipline, or sila paramita, clearly. It becomes the basis of everything. It is, one might say, the narrow path, which is in itself a kind of simplicity. For instance, if there was only one little track through a mountain pass and the rest of the terrain was completely overgrown with trees and bushes and so on, then we would have no difficulty at all in deciding which way to go. If there is only one track, either you go on or you turn back. The whole thing is simplified into one event, or one continuity. Therefore discipline does not limit our activities by declaring that such-and-such a thing is against the divine law or is immoral; it is just that there is only one way of true simplicity ahead of us. Fundamentally, discipline comes down to the shamatha practice of developing awareness, through which one merely sees what is. Every moment is now, and one acts through the experience of the present moment. We have now talked of the narrow path.

From there we come to the Mahayana, the "Great Vehicle," which is the open path, the path of the bodhisattva. The narrow path is not merely simple and direct, but also has great character, great dignity.

Building on that foundation we develop
compassion. In reality compassion has
nothing particularly to do with being compassionate, in the sense of being charitable
or kind to one's neighbors or giving regular donations to refugees or paying sub-
scriptions to various charitable organiza-
tions, although that may also be included.
This charity is fundamental; it amounts to
developing warmth within oneself. Out of
his simplicity and awareness the bodhisattva develops selfless warmth. He doesn't
even think in terms of his own psychological benefit; he doesn't think, "*I* would like
to see him not suffering." "*I*" does not
come into it at all. He speaks and thinks
and acts spontaneously, not thinking even
in terms of helping, or fulfilling any particular purpose. He does not act on "religious" or "charitable" grounds at all. He
just acts according to the true, present
moment, through which he develops a
kind of warmth. And there is a great

warmth in this awareness and also great creativity. His actions are not limited by anything, and all sorts of creative impulses just arise in him and are somehow exactly right for that particular moment. Things just happen and he simply sails through them, so there is a continual, tremendous creativity in him. That is the real act of karuna—a Sanskrit word which means "noble heart" or "compassionate heart." So in this case compassion does not refer to kindness alone, but to fundamental compassion, selfless compassion. He is not really aware of *himself,* so compassion has greater scope to expand and develop, because here there is no radiator but only radiation. And when only this radiation exists, without a radiator, it could go on and on and on, and the energy would never be used up. It is always transformed and as it expands further and further it changes always into something else, into a new creative activity, so it goes continuously on and on. This creative transformation is not merely a theoretical or philosophical concept, but actually takes place in a practical sense, sometimes in a very simple way.

We can turn now to generosity, which arises when the bodhisattva is intoxicated by compassion and is no longer aware of himself. His mind is not merely filled with compassion, it becomes compassion, it *is* compassion. There are six activities associated with this: generosity, morality or discipline (spontaneous discipline, acting according to the true law), patience, energy and clarity (which is also wisdom or knowing the situation). These are what is known as the paramitas which, as we said, means transcendent acts. Let me repeat that the bodhisattva is not acting to be virtuous or to overcome sin or evil; his mind is not occupied with being on the side of good or bad. In other words his activity is not limited, it is not bound or conditioned by good and bad. Hence it is transcendental, something beyond. This may sound a bit abstract, a bit difficult to grasp, and one may ask, "How can an act of generosity be transcendental? Isn't this merely a philosophical definition?" Well, no, in this case it isn't, because it does not refer only to his action. His mind simply doesn't work like that. When he acts he is completely spontaneous, free and being-in-the-present. So he is entirely open and, as far as his mind is concerned, nonactive. Activity arises only when the situation presents itself. He may not be continually in a state of selfless awareness, but at least he acts spontaneously, he acts according to the Dharma. And the definition of Dharma in this sense is the true law, the law of the universe. Dispassion is the Dharma. That is to say that the Dharma does not involve any form of desire for achievement, so the act of generosity is performed without reference to any particular reward. Therefore generosity means not possessing.

If a man has wealth he might say, "Well, now I have an opportunity to practice generosity because I have something to practice with." But for the bodhisattva this question doesn't arise at all; it is not a question of owning anything. Generosity is simply an attitude of mind in which one does not want to possess and then distribute among people. Again, generosity refers not only to the practice of meditation, where one may feel a kind of selflessness of not holding anything back, but it is also something positive. In the scriptures Buddha speaks of the practice of generosity by stretching the arm out and by holding the arm in. There is a story from the time of Buddha of a beggar woman who was one of the poorest beggars in India, because she was poor in kind and also poor in mind. She wanted so much, and this made her feel even poorer. One day she heard that Buddha was invited to Anathapindika's place in the Jeta Grove. Anathapindika was a wealthy householder and a great donor. So she decided to follow Buddha because she knew that he would give her food, whatever was left over. She attended the ceremony of offering food to the sangha, to Buddha, and then she sat there waiting until Buddha saw her. He turned around and asked her, "What do you want?" Of course he knew, but she actually had to admit and say it. And she said, "I want food. I want you to give me what is left over." And Buddha said, "In that case you must first say no. You have to refuse when I offer it to you." He held out the food to her, but she found it very difficult to say no. She realized that in all her life she had never said no. Whenever anyone had anything or offered her anything, she had always said, "Yes, I want it." So she found it very difficult to say no, as she was not at all familiar with that word. After great difficulty she finally did say no, and then Buddha gave her the food. And through this she realized that the real hunger inside her was the desire to own, grasp, possess and want. This is an example of how one can practice generosity. And from that point of view one can practice generosity toward oneself, because the point here is to free oneself from this possessiveness, this continual wanting.

Then, of course, the next step is giving away one's possessions. But this is not necessarily connected with austerity. It does not mean that you should not own anything at all or that you should give away what you have immediately. You could have great wealth and many possessions and you could even enjoy them and like having them and probably you have a personal interest in them—like a child's toy, or adult's toy for that matter. It isn't a question of not seeing the value of possessions, the point is that it should be equally easy to give them away. If somebody asks for a particular object that you like to have with you all the time, there should be no hesitation at all, just give it away. It is really a question of giving up this concept of possession. For there is a kind of hunger in action.

There is a story in Tibet concerning two brothers, one of whom had ninety-nine yaks while the other had only one yak. The poor brother was quite content with his one yak. He was quite happy and thought he had great wealth. He had one yak and that was really all he needed. It was quite sufficient and he wasn't particularly afraid of losing it. In fact his enjoyment of owning it was greater than his fear of losing it, whereas the other one was always very afraid of losing his yaks. He always had to look after them, and generally you find in the highlands of Tibet that there are a lot of wolves and Himalayan mountain bears, and the yaks quite often die through the hardships of winter. There are far more obstacles there than in this part of the world when it comes to looking after animals. So one day the rich brother thought, "Well, I think I'll ask my brother a favor." You see, he was not only afraid of losing his yaks, he was also very keen on accumulating more of them. And he went to the other brother and said, "Well, I know you have only one yak, which doesn't make much difference to you. So if you didn't have one at all it wouldn't really matter very much. But if you give me your yak then I will have a hundred yaks, which means a great deal to me. I mean a hundred yaks is really something. If I had that much I would really be somebody rich and famous." So he asked the favor. And the other brother gave up the yak quite easily. He didn't hesitate; he just gave it. And this story became proverbial in Tibet to illustrate that when someone has a lot he wants more, and when someone has less he is prepared to give.

So there is this possessiveness, this psy-

chological hunger. And this relates not
only to money and wealth but to the deep-
seated feeling of wanting to possess, wanting to hold on to things, wanting things
definitely to belong to you. For example,
supposing you are window shopping. One
person might be unhappy all the time, and
when he sees things he likes, this always
produces a kind of pain in his mind because he is thinking, "If only I had the
money, I could buy that!" So all the time
as he is walking through the shops this
hunger produces great pain. Whereas another person may enjoy merely looking. So
this wanting to own, wanting to possess
and not being prepared to give out, is not
really a weakness for any particular thing.
It is more generally wanting to occupy
oneself with something, and if you have
lost or lose interest in that particular
thing, then you always want to substitute
something else in its place. It isn't particularly that you can't manage without a

motor car or central heating or whatever it may be. There is always something behind that, something fundamental, a kind of wanting to possess, wanting to own, which is always changing and developing and substituting one thing for another. So that is the real weakness—though not exactly weakness, but more a kind of habit that one tends to form through a neurotic process of thoughts. The whole thing boils down to this overlapping of thoughts which goes on all the time in our minds. We never allow anything to really happen or take place in our mind. One thought comes and almost before we finish that another one comes in and overlaps it and then another. So we never allow any gap which would permit us to be free and really digest things. Therefore it becomes a continual demand, a continual process of creating and wanting to own. And that is why one has to develop this generosity of really opening oneself.

The next stage is perhaps a deeper form of generosity. That is to say, being prepared to share one's experience with others. Now that is a rather tricky thing because there is also a danger that you will be trying to teach somebody else what you have learned. It is rather a delicate matter. You might reveal something partly because you would like to talk about it. It may be rather exciting and perhaps you know more about it than the other person and want to show off. This is a bit tricky. Nevertheless, putting it into words — whatever you have achieved — and giving it to someone else, is the only way to develop yourself. This particularly applies to teachers. And for advanced teachers, in fact for any teachers, it is necessary not just to learn things and keep them, but to use them and put them into effect by giving them out, though not with the idea of any reward. That is what is known as the dana of Dharma, where you give out all the time.

Of course you have to be very careful not to give the wrong present to the wrong person. Supposing, for example, that the person is not very keen on listening to your experiences, particularly connected with meditation and so on, then you do not go on talking about it, because then it would not really be dana at all. And perhaps to such a person it would be more appropriate to give something else rather than Dharma. And one has to see that with intelligence, clarity and wisdom; the prajna paramita will have to deal with that. But on the whole one has to give out if one wants to receive anything in. A continual process of transformation takes place.

There is a tradition in Tibet that if you want to receive any teaching or instruction, you generally give some present to the guru. This does not mean, by the way, that I want to collect from the audience. But the concept behind this is that when you want something—"I would like to re-

ceive teaching. I want to know something"—then you have to give out something as well. This also raises the point that
you are not entirely a poor person who is
dependent on somebody or humiliated because you just want help, but you have
something great to give out. In the Tibetan
tradition of Buddhism, when people went
to India to translate texts and receive
teachings from Indian masters, they spent
first about two years collecting gold from
all over Tibet. They always gave something
before they received instruction. So the
whole point there is that one has to realize
the value of teachings, though one can't
really price them at all in terms of material
wealth. But one must be prepared to give
out something, and one of the most important things of all, of course, is giving
out ego, which is one of our most precious
and valuable possessions. We have to give
that out. And there are certain practices,
such as prostrations, in the Tibetan tradi-

tion, where before one can practice any of the further stages of meditation one has to do a hundred thousand prostrations—this is in connection with the practice of Buddhist yoga. And the idea of prostration is giving out, surrendering, opening—a kind of emptying-out process, or preparation of the vessel or container, in order to receive. You have to open and empty out an already sound cup. That is what you have to offer, and then you can receive everything intact with complete value, with complete quality.

In the case of a teacher, of course, that is also very important, and I am sure we are all teachers in our different ways, I am sure we can always teach people in different degrees. And teachers must be prepared to learn from pupils, that is very, very important. Otherwise there is really no progress on the part of the students, because in a sense one would be too keen and interested in the process of making the pupils receive the expansion of one's own ego and wanting to produce another you, rather than helping them to develop ability of their own. So teachers must be prepared to learn from their pupils, then there is a continual rapport. Exchanging takes place all the time; then as you teach, the pupils don't get bored with you, because you develop as well. There is always something different, something new each moment, so the material never runs out. One could apply this even to technical studies and the way of teaching things. It could be mathematics or science or anything at all. If the teacher is prepared to learn from the pupil, then the pupil also becomes eager to give, so there is real love, and real communication takes place. That is the greatest generosity. One can see in the life of Buddha that he never taught merely with a kind of pompous authority. He never just used his authority as Buddha, as the awakened person. He never taught

by saying, "You are wrong and I am right."
Though he did sometimes point out that
this is the right path and that is wrong,
using discriminative wisdom, but somehow
he always encouraged discussions among
his disciples. And the disciples always con-
tributed something to his teaching, and he
always communicated in a certain way and
asked certain questions; "Is that so, or is it
not?" And judgment was left to the pupils.
And then he said "Yes" or "No," but
whatever the answer was he just built from
there. So a continual give-and-take process
took place, and I am sure one can also do
this in a very similar way. Of course, when
one has something to say, one would generally like to just read straight through before getting any criticisms or any kind of
reaction from the other person, which is
really based on a kind of secret fear, not
being fully confident in oneself because
one is afraid to show the folly of ego. So
one tends to state it as a bald fact and just

leave it. Then, when the pupil can't quite take part in it, it becomes very formal and very difficult and solemn and they don't enjoy learning. They become conscious of being taught, of being told this and that, and then somehow it ceases to be creative and it doesn't really seep into their personality and enable them to develop their own ability and knowledge.

Then of course generosity of material wealth, as we have said, is not merely a question of giving the object or giving money, but more of the attitude behind it. One generally finds in the East — and I am not saying that the Eastern way of doing things is always right, I am not using it as a kind of authority as though that is the authentic and only way to deal with things, but merely as another suggestion — that a person in the East will generally give a thing away because that is the thing he loves most, and he gives it because it really represents his heart. It is most strange the things that happen in the case of someone like myself, having been abbot of a monastery traveling round in various districts of Tibet. One has been given all sorts of things such as headdresses and ornaments, women's aprons and women's shoes and rings and so on. Not that they thought one really needed these things, but it was their precious object, something which in fact represented them. They have in them this desire to possess and that is why they give in this way. The giving and the concept of punya, merit, is not just a question of giving objects and spending a large sum of money, but also of taking part in it physically and being wholly involved in the process of giving. As with anything else in this kind of work, such as the practice of meditation, you have to be fully involved, you have to become one with what you are doing. So it is with giving things away, no matter how small the thing is in terms of value, one must be fully involved in the giving so that a part of one's ego is also given away. Through that one reaches the paramita, the transcendental act, which is something beyond. Then one is not conscious of "virtue" and giving away things in an effort to be "religious," and one is not conscious of receiving any particular reward of good merit. If one is giving merely in order to gain merit, then that tends to build up one's ego rather than really giving anything away. So if one is able to give out one's self, ego, a part of that possessiveness and passion, then one is really practicing the Dharma, which is passionlessness, and the merit automatically becomes a by-product, and one is not all the time trying to achieve merit.

PATIENCE

Patience, ksanti in Sanskrit, is usually taken to mean forbearance and the calm endurance of pain and hardship. But in fact it means rather more than that. It is forbearing in the sense of seeing the situation and seeing that it is right to forbear and to develop patience. So ksanti has an aspect of intelligence in contrast, one might say, to an animal loaded with baggage which might still go on and on walking along the track until it just drops dead. That kind of patience is patience without wisdom, without clarity. Here we are referring to patience with clarity, and energy with the eye of understanding. Generally when we talk of patience we think of an individual person who is being patient, but it also has a great deal to do with communication. Patience can develop if there is discipline and if one can create the right situation. Then one does not merely forbear because it is painful and unpleasant and because one is just trying to get through it, but patience can develop easily with the aid of virya, or energy. Without energy one could not develop patience because there would be no strength to be patient, and this energy comes from creating the right situation, which is connected with awareness. Perhaps the word *awareness* is a little ambiguous, since it often connotes self-consciousness or just being aware of what you are doing, but in this case awareness is simply seeing the situation accurately. It does not particularly mean watching yourself speaking and acting, but rather seeing the situation as a whole, like an aerial view of a landscape which reveals the layout of the town and so on. So patience is related to discipline, which in turn is connected with awareness.

Discipline is in fact the key to everything, and sila, morality, is the source of discipline and the main function of discipline. And here there are two schools of thought: according to one, discipline is necessary and only through discipline can one learn and find the right way; according to the other school of thought, things should be allowed to develop in their own way, and if there is less discipline, if things are left to the individual's choice or instinct, then he will develop a personal interest in the subject and there will be no need to impose anything on him. Both are extreme views. Not that Buddhists like to compromise in every case; it is more a question of seeing things very clearly. Whenever there is too much discipline it is invariably being imposed by someone else. There are rules and regulations, and one is always being watched and told what to do, in which case one is not really being what one is — somebody else is merely expanding his ego and imposing his idea on you. That would be a kind of dictatorship rather than discipline, because it would be trying to force things to grow, as opposed to allowing them to grow naturally. On the other hand, if discipline is left entirely to the individual and he has to feel his own way, he would find it very difficult — except in the very rare case of a person who is very intelligent and highly controlled, in the sense of not being influenced by an irregular or neurotic pattern of thoughts, opinions and emotions. Which is not to say that most people are mad or psychologically disturbed but this element is in everyone. There is usually a neurotic aspect which causes us in some way or another to react to a given situation and develop a neurotic way of dealing with it, which is not at all the true way. That is acting according to one's conditioning rather than according to what *is*. So in this case the person would not have the ability to develop freedom because freedom is not properly presented to him. Freedom must be presented properly. In fact the word *freedom* itself is a relative term: freedom *from* something, otherwise there is no freedom. And since it is freedom from something, one must first create the right situation, which is patience.

This kind of freedom cannot be created by an outsider or some superior authority. One must develop the ability to know the situation. In other words, one has to develop a panoramic awareness, an all-pervading awareness, knowing the situation *at that very moment.* It is a question of knowing the situation and opening one's eyes to that very moment of nowness, and this is not particularly a mystical experience or anything mysterious at all, but just direct, open and clear perception of what *is now*. And when a person is able to see what *is now* without being influenced by the past or any expectation of the future, but just seeing the very moment of now, then at that moment there is no barrier at all. For a barrier could only arise from association with the past or expectation of the future. So the present moment has no barriers at all. And then he finds there is a tremendous energy in him, a tremendous strength to practice patience. He becomes like a warrior. When a warrior goes to war he does not think of the past or his previous experience of war, nor does he think of the consequences for the future; he just sails through it and fights, and that is the right way to be a warrior. Similarly, when there is a tremendous conflict going on, one has to develop this energy combined with patience. And this is what is known as right patience with the all-seeing eye, patience with clarity.

Of course, one may find it possible to be open and mindful of the present moment when one is alone or when the right situation presents itself—say, on a sunny

day or a pleasant evening, or in good company, or reading a suitable book or something of that nature, where the situation is
right or closer to what one wants to do—
then it is easier. But often it does not happen like that. Perhaps one is in the wrong
company, or perhaps one is terribly de-
pressed or very disturbed in some way, but
one has to see the sameness of the two
aspects. Of course, this is very easy to talk
about and rather difficult to do. The thing
is that even when the situation appears to
be favorable, such as right here in the
country where everything is quiet and
there is no noise, still one is somehow
never able to escape from emotional dis-
turbances and depression and the great
collection of things in one's mind. Partly
these are interdependent with other people, and partly it is because one is not able
to be open and develop enough strength of
patience. Therefore the whole thing tends
to split off as a separate entity rather than

being a part of the whole pattern of a mandala. That is to say that one should always remain in the center and not react to the situation. If one thinks something is going wrong and one would like to see it done right, that may be a very charitable thought; nevertheless there is the element of "I" involved: " 'I' would like him to be happy," or "If it makes him happy then I will be happy as well," so there is the idea of both enjoying this happiness. And either way this is a kind of indulging in happiness. So it often occurs that one is not being in the center of the potter's wheel, as it were, and if one accidentally throws clay on the edge of a potter's wheel, it flies off. There is nothing wrong with the clay and nothing wrong with the wheel; you simply threw the clay in the wrong spot. And if you throw the clay in the center, then it makes beautiful pots. So the whole point is that you have to be in the center all the time and not expect some external person or situation to act for you. In other words, he who develops highly skilled patience will never expect anything from anyone, not because he is distrustful, but because he knows how to be at the center and he *is* the center. So in order to achieve silence you would not chase the birds away because they make a noise. In order to be still you would not stop the movement of air or the rushing river, but accept them and you will yourself be aware of the silence. Just accept them as part of the establishment of silence. So the mental aspect of the noise of birds affects the psychological aspect in you. In other words, the noise that birds make is one factor, and one's psychological concept of noise is another. And when one can deal with that side, the noise of birds becomes merely audible silence. So the whole point is that one should not expect anything from outside, one should not try to change the other person or try to put across one's opinions. One should not try to convince a person at the wrong moment, when one knows he already has a very clear idea of his own, or it is simply not the right moment for your words to get through to him. There is an analogy of two people walking barefoot along a very rough road, and one thought it would be very good to cover the whole road with leather so it would be very soft, but the other one, who was wiser, said, "No, I think if we covered our feet with leather that would be the same." So that is patience, which is not being distrustful, but is a matter of not expecting anything and not trying to change the situation outside oneself. And that is the only way to create peace in the world. If you yourself are prepared to step into it and to accept, then somebody else makes the same contribution. So if a hundred people did the same the whole thing would become right.

There is a Tibetan story that there were

once a hundred and one soldiers, and one of them, who was quite young, happened to be the son of the commander-in-chief. And his father said to him, "You seem to be late. All the others have saddled their horses, so how about you?" And he answered and said, "Well, if a hundred people can saddle their hundred horses so quickly, then one person will not take very long." But of course they had all saddled their horses at the same time, so he was left behind. So if one expects the external situation to change, the whole thing becomes reversed and one finds that from all directions one is being pushed away and one is being defeated. It is like walking on ice. Sometimes, of course, one can change the situation with certain people—perhaps by going through a series of painful steps, like complaining to the person or going to great lengths to explain that so-and-so disturbs one, or such-and-such a thing is not acceptable. But by the time one has gone through this rather long process, the very aim one was trying to achieve—namely peace and quiet—has long ago disappeared, and one hasn't achieved anything. So the whole thing becomes a continual rat race. Therefore patience is the way to set the example of peace. If one would like to create a quiet atmosphere somewhere, then one has to develop patience—not just bearing pain, but seeing the amusing side of that situation where one finds oneself irritated. And if one is able to see that particular aspect, the ironical aspect (which is also an interesting aspect), then somehow the situation is no longer irritating and no longer intrudes on our property of silence. If one is able to accept it in a relaxed way, a quiet way, that is already the first step in producing a climate of peace and an atmosphere of quiet, and then somebody might feel that, even without saying it.

So patience is the key to the develop-

'ment of an open center and the establishment of a stable base for the practice of
meditation. Moreover, it is very important
in dealing with life, in dealing with people
and for living in the world in which you
have to live. For most people patience has
a rather different connotation, almost puritanical, of being cool and naive and not
saying very much: life may be painful, but
one just bears it with a false smile. And
that is not patience at all, because if one is
not prepared to be one with the situation
and see the amusing aspect, then one day
this puritanical forbearance is bound to
break, it is bound to burst, and then there
would be no place for patience at all.

MEDITATION

Meditation is a vast subject and there have been many developments throughout the ages and many variations among the different religious traditions. But broadly speaking the basic character of meditation takes one of two forms. The first stems from the teachings which are concerned with the discovery of the nature of existence; the second concerns communication with the external or universal concept of God. In either case meditation is the only way to put the teachings into practice.

Where there is the concept of an external, "higher" Being, there is also an internal personality — which is known as "I" or the ego. In this case meditation practice becomes a way of developing communication with an external Being. This means that one feels oneself to be inferior and one is trying to contact something higher, greater. Such meditation is based on devotion. This is basically an inward or introverted practice of meditation, which is well known in the Hindu teachings where the emphasis is on going into the inward state of samadhi, into the depths of the heart. One finds a similar technique practiced in the Orthodox teachings of Christianity, where the prayer of the heart is used and concentration on the heart is emphasized. This is a means of identifying oneself with an external Being and necessitates purifying oneself. The basic belief is that one is separate from God, but there is still a link, one is still part of God. This confusion sometimes arises, and in order to clarify it one has to work inward and try to raise the standard of individuality to the level of a higher consciousness. This approach makes use of emotions and devotional practices which are aimed at making contact with God or gods or some particular saint. These devotional practices may also include the recitation of mantra.

The other principal form of meditation is almost entirely opposite in its approach, though finally it might lead to the same results. Here there is no belief in higher and lower; the idea of different levels, or of being in an underdeveloped state, does not arise. One does not feel inferior, and what one is trying to achieve is not something higher than oneself. Therefore the practice of meditation does not require an inward concentration on the heart. There is no centralizing concept at all. Even such practices as concentrating on the chakras, or psychic centers of the body, are approached in a different way. Although in certain teachings of Buddhism the concept of chakras is mentioned, the practices connected with them are not based on the development of an inward center. So this basic form of meditation is concerned with trying to see what *is*. There are many variations on this form of meditation, but they are generally based on various techniques for opening oneself. The achievement of this kind of meditation is not, therefore, the result of some long-term, arduous practice through which we build ourselves up into a "higher" state, nor does it necessitate going into any kind of inner trance state. It is rather what one might call "working meditation" or extrovert meditation, where skillful means and wisdom must be combined like the two wings of a bird. This is not a question of trying to retreat from the world. In fact without the external world, the world of apparent phenomena, meditation would be almost impossible to practice, for the individual and the external world are not separate, but merely coexist together. Therefore the concept of trying to communicate and trying to become one with some higher Being does not arise.

In this kind of meditation practice the

concept of *nowness* plays a very important part. In fact, it is the essence of meditation. Whatever one does, whatever one tries to practice, is not aimed at achieving a higher state or at following some theory or ideal, but simply, without any object or ambition, trying to see what is here and now. One has to become aware of the present moment through such means as concentrating on the breathing, a practice which has been developed in the Buddhist tradition. This is based on developing the knowledge of nowness, for each respiration is unique, it is an expression of *now*. Each breath is separate from the next and is fully seen and fully felt, not in a visualized form, nor simply as an aid to concentration, but it should be fully and properly dealt with. Just as a very hungry man, when he is eating, is not even conscious that he is eating food. He is so engrossed in the food that he completely identifies himself with what he is doing and almost becomes one with the taste and enjoyment of it. Similarly with the breathing, the whole idea is to try and see through that very moment in time. So in this case the concept of trying to become something higher does not arise at all, and opinions do not have much importance. In a sense opinions provide a way to escape; they create a kind of slothfulness and obscure one's clarity of vision. The clarity of our consciousness is veiled by prefabricated concepts and whatever we see we try to fit into some pigeonhole or in some way make it fit in with our preconceived ideas. So concepts and theories—and, for that matter, theology—can become obstacles. One might ask, therefore, what is the point of studying Buddhist philosophy? Since there are scriptures and texts and there is surely some philosophy to believe in, wouldn't that also be a concept? Well, that depends on the individual, but basically it is not so. From the start one tries to transcend concepts, and one tries, perhaps in a very critical way, to find out what *is*. One has to develop a critical mind which will stimulate intelligence. This may at first cause one to reject what is said by teachers or what is written in books, but then gradually one begins to feel something and to find something for oneself. That is what is known as the meeting of imagination and reality, where the feeling of certain words and concepts meets with intuitive knowledge, perhaps in a rather vague and imprecise way. One may be uncertain whether what one is learning is right or not, but there is a general feeling that one is about to discover something. One cannot really start by being perfect, but one must start with something. And if one cultivates this intelligent, intuitive insight, then gradually, stage by stage, the real intuitive feeling develops and the imaginary or hallucinatory element is gradually clarified and eventually dies out.

Finally that vague feeling of discovery becomes very clear, so that almost no doubt remains. Even at this stage it is possible that one may be unable to explain one's discovery verbally or write it down exactly on paper, and in fact if one tried to do so it would be limiting one's scope and would be rather dangerous. Nevertheless, as this feeling grows and develops one finally attains direct knowledge, rather than achieving something which is separate from oneself. As in the analogy of the hungry man, you become one with the subject. This can only be achieved through the practice of meditation. Therefore meditation is very much a matter of exercise — it is a working practice. It is not a question of going into some inward depth, but of widening and expanding outward.

These are the basic differences between the two types of meditation practice. The first may be more suitable for some people and the second may be more suitable for others. It is not a question of one being superior or more accurate than the other. But for any form of meditation one must first overcome that great feeling of demand and ambition which acts as a major obstacle. Making demands on a person, such as a guru, or having the ambition to achieve something out of what one is doing, arises out of a built-up desire or wantingness; and that wantingness is a centralized notion. This centralized notion is basically blind. It is like having only one eye, and that one eye being situated in the chest. When you try to walk you cannot turn your head around and you can only see a limited area. Because you can see in only one direction the intelligence of turning the head is lacking. Therefore there is a great danger of falling. This wantingness acts as a veil and becomes an obstacle to the discovery of the moment of nowness, because the wanting is based either on the future or on trying to continue something which existed in the past, so the nowness is completely forgotten. There may be a certain effort to focus on the nowness, but perhaps only twenty percent of the consciousness is based on the present and the rest is scattered into the past or the future. Therefore there is not enough force to see directly what is there.

Here, too, the teaching of selflessness plays a very important part. This is not merely a question of denying the existence of ego, for ego is something relative. Where there is an external person, a higher being, or the concept of something which is separate from oneself, then we tend to think that because there is something outside there must be something here as well. The external phenomenon sometimes becomes such an overwhelming thing and seems to have all sorts of seductive or aggressive qualities, so we erect a kind of defense mechanism against it, failing to see that that is itself a continuity of the external thing. We try to segregate ourselves from the external, and this creates a kind of gigantic bubble in us which consists of nothing but air and water or, in this case, fear and the reflection of the external thing. So this huge bubble prevents any fresh air from coming in, and that is "I"—the ego. So in that sense there is the existence of the ego, but it is in fact illusory. Having established that, one generally wants to create some external idol or refuge. Subconsciously one knows that this "I" is only a bubble and it could burst at any moment, so one tries to protect it as much as one can—either consciously or subconsciously. In fact we have achieved such skill at protecting this ego that we have managed to preserve it for hundreds of years. It is as though a person has a very precious pair of spectacles which he puts in a box or various containers in order to keep it safe, so that even if other things are broken this would be preserved. He may feel that other things could bear hardship, but he knows that this could not, so this would last longer. In the same way, ego lasts longer just because one feels it could burst at any time. There is fear of it being destroyed because that would be too much, one would feel too exposed. And there is such character, such a fascinating pattern established outside us, although it is in fact our own reflection. That is why the concept of egolessness is not really a question of whether there is a self or not, or, for that matter, whether there is the existence of God or not; it is rather the taking away of that concept of the bubble. Having done so, one doesn't have to deliberately destroy the ego or deliberately condemn God. And when that barrier is removed one can expand and swim through straightaway. But this can only be achieved through the practice of meditation, which must be approached in a very practical and simple way. Then the mystical experience of joy or grace, or whatever it might be, can be found in every object. That is what one tries to achieve through vipassana, or "insight" meditation practice. Once we have established a basic pattern of discipline and we have developed a regular way of dealing with the situation—whether it is breathing or walking or what have you—then at some stage the technique gradually dies out. Reality gradually expands so that we do not have to use the technique at all. And in this case one does not have to concentrate inward, but one can expand outward more and more. And the more one expands, the closer one gets to the realization of centerless existence.

That is the basic pattern of this kind of meditation, which is based on three fundamental factors: first, not centralizing inward; second, not having any longing to become higher; and third, becoming completely identified with here and now. These three elements run right through the practice of meditation, from the beginning up to the moment of realization.

Q. You mentioned nowness in your talk, and I was wondering how it is possible to become aware of the absolute through awareness of a relative moment in time?

A. Well, we have to start by working through the relative aspect, until finally this nowness takes on such a living quality that it is no longer dependent on a relative way of expressing nowness. One might say that *now* exists all the time, beyond the concept of relativity. But since all concepts are based on the idea of relativity, it is impossible to find any words which go beyond that. So nowness is the only way to see directly. First it is between the past and the future—now. Then gradually one discovers that nowness is not dependent on relativity at all. One discovers that the past does not exist, the future does not exist, and everything happens now. Similarly, in order to express space one might have first to create a vase, and then one has to break it, and then one sees that the emptiness in the vase is the same as the emptiness outside. That is the whole meaning of technique. At first that nowness is, in a sense, not perfect. Or one might even say that the meditation is not perfect, it is a purely man-made practice. One sits and tries to be still and concentrates on the breathing, and so on. But then, having started in that way, one gradually discovers something more than that. So the effort one has put into it — into the discovery of nowness, for example — would not be wasted, though at the same time one might see that it was rather foolish. But that is the only way to start.

Q. For meditation, would a student have to rid himself of ego before he started, or would this come naturally as he is studying?

A. This comes naturally, because you

can't start without ego. And basically ego isn't bad. Good and bad doesn't really exist anywhere, it is only a secondary thing. Ego is, in a sense, a false thing, but it isn't necessarily bad. You have to start with ego, and use ego, and from there it gradually wears out, like a pair of shoes. But you have to use it and wear it out thoroughly, so it is not preserved. Otherwise, if you try to push ego aside and start perfect, you may become more and more perfect in a rather one-sided way, but the same amount of imperfection is building up on the other side, just as creating intense light creates intense darkness as well.

Q. You mentioned that there are two basic forms of meditation—devotional practice, or trying to communicate with something higher, and the other one, which is simply awareness of what is—but this devotional practice still plays a part in Buddhism as well, and you have devotional chants and so on, so I am not quite sure how this comes in. I mean, the two appear to be different, so can they in fact be combined?

A. Yes, but the kind of devotional practice which is found in Buddhism is merely a process of opening, of surrendering the ego. It is a process of creating a container. I don't mean to condemn the other kind of devotion, but if one looks at it from the point of view of a person who has an unskillful way of using that technique, then devotion becomes a longing to free oneself. One sees oneself as being very separate, and as being imprisoned and imperfect. One regards oneself as basically bad, and one is trying to break out. In other words the imperfection part of oneself is identified with "I" and anything perfect is identified with some external being, so all that is left is trying to get through the imprisonment. This kind of devotion is an overemphasized awareness of ego, the negative aspect of ego. Although there are hundreds of variations of devotional practice in Buddhism, and there are many accounts of devotion to gurus, or being able to communicate with the guru, and of achieving the awakened state of mind through devotion. But in these cases devotion is always begun without centralizing on the ego. In any chants or ceremonies, for example, which make use of symbolism, or the visualization of Buddhas, before any visualization is created there is first a formless meditation, which creates an entirely open space. And at the end one always recites what is known as the Threefold Wheel: "I do not exist; the external visualization does not exist; and the act of visualizing does not exist"—the idea being that any feeling of achievement is thrown back to the openness, so one doesn't feel that one is collecting anything. I think that is the basic point. One may feel a great deal of devotion, but that devotion is a kind of abstract form of devotion, which does not centralize inwardly. One simply identifies with that feeling of devotion, and that's all. This is perhaps a different concept of devotion, where no center exists, but only devotion exists. Whereas, in the other case devotion contains a demand. There is an expectation of getting something out of it in return.

Q. Is there not a great fear generated when we get to this point of opening up and surrendering?

A. Fear is one of the weapons of ego. It protects the ego. If one reaches the stage where one begins to see the folly of ego, then there is fear of losing the ego, and fear is one of its last weapons. Beyond that point fear no longer exists, because the object of fear is to frighten somebody, and when that somebody is not there, then fear loses its function. You see, fear is continually given life by your response, and when there is no one to respond to the fear—which is ego loss—then fear ceases to exist.

Q. You are talking about the ego as an object?

A. In what sense?

Q. In the sense that it is part of the external environment.

A. Ego is, as I have already said, like a bubble. It is an object up to a point, because although it does not really exist—it is an impermanent thing—it in fact shows itself as an object more than actually being one. That is another way of protecting oneself, of trying to maintain ego.

Q. This is an aspect of the ego?

A. Yes.

Q. Then you can't destroy the ego, or you would lose the power to recognize, the power to cognate.

A. No, not necessarily. Because ego does not contain understanding, it does not contain any insight at all. Ego exists in a false way all the time and can only create confusion, whereas insight is something more than that.

Q. Would you say that ego is a secondary phenomenon rather than a primary phenomenon?

A. Yes, very much so. In a sense ego is wisdom, but ego happens to be ignorant as well. You see, when you realize that you are ignorant, that is the beginning of the discovery of wisdom—it is wisdom itself.

Q. How does one decide in oneself whether ego is ignorance or wisdom?

A. It is not really a question of deciding. It is simply that one sees in that way. You see, basically there is no solid substance, although we talk about ego existing as a solid thing having various aspects. But in fact it merely lives through time as a continual process of creation. It is continually dying and being reborn all the time. Therefore ego doesn't really exist. But ego also acts as a kind of wisdom: when ego dies, that is wisdom itself, and when ego is first formulated that is the beginning of ignorance itself. So wisdom and ego are not really separate at all. It seems rather difficult to define, and in a way one would be happier if there was clear-cut black and white, but somehow that is not the natural pattern of existence. There is no clear-cut black and white at all, and all things are interdependent. Darkness is an aspect of light, and light is an aspect of darkness, so one can't really condemn one side and build up everything on the other. It is left entirely to the individual to find his own way, and it is possible to do so. It is the same for a dog who has never swum—if he was suddenly thrown in the water he could swim. Similarly, we have a kind of spiritual instinct in us and if we are willing to open ourselves then somehow we find our way directly. It is only a question of opening up and one doesn't have to have a clear-cut definition at all.

Q. Would you care to sum up the purpose of meditation?

A. Well, meditation is dealing with purpose itself. It is not that meditation is for something, but it is dealing with the aim. Generally we have a purpose for whatever we do: something is going to happen in the future, therefore what I am doing now is important—everything is related to that. But the whole idea of meditation is to develop an entirely different way of dealing with things, where you have no purpose at all. In fact meditation is dealing with the question of whether or not there is such a thing as purpose. And when one learns a different way of dealing with the situation, one no longer has to have a purpose. One is not on the way to somewhere. Or rather, one is on the way and one is also at the destination at the same time. That is really what meditation is for.

Q. Would you say, then, that it would be a merging with reality?

A. Yes, because reality is there all the time. Reality is not a separate entity, so it is a question of becoming one with reality, or of being in reality—not *achieving* oneness, but becoming identified with it. One is already a part of that reality, so all that remains is to take away the doubt. Then one discovers that one has been there all the time.

Q. Would it be correct to describe it as the realization that the visible is not reality?

A. The visible? Can you define a bit more?

Q. I am thinking of William Blake's theory of the merging of the observer with the observed, and the visible not being the reality at all.

A. Visible things in this sense are reality. There is nothing beyond nowness, therefore what we see is reality. But because of our usual way of seeing things, we do not see them exactly as they are.

Q. Would you say, then, that each person is an individual and must find an individual way towards that?

A. Well, I think that brings us back to the question of ego, which we have been talking about. You see, there is such a thing as personality, in a way, but we are not really individuals as separate from the environment, or as separate from external phenomena. That is why a different approach is necessary. Whereas, if we were individuals and had no connection with the rest of things, then there would be no need for a different technique which would lead to oneness. The point is that there is appearance of individuality, but this individuality is based on relativity. If there is individuality, there must also be oneness as well.

Q. Yes, but it is the individuality that makes for oneness. If we weren't individuals we couldn't be one. Is that so?

A. Well, the word "individual" is rather

ambiguous. At the beginning individuality may be overemphasized, because there are various individual aspects. Even when we reach the stage of realization there is perhaps an element of compassion, an element of wisdom, an element of energy and all sorts of different variations. But what we describe as an individual is something more than that. We tend to see it as one character with many things built onto it, which is a way of trying to find some sort of security. When there is wisdom, we try to load everything onto it, and it then becomes an entirely separate entity, a separate person—which is not so. But still there are individual aspects, there is individual character. So in Hinduism one finds different aspects of God, different deities and different symbols. When one attains oneness with reality, that reality is not just one single thing, but one can see from a very wide angle.

Q. If a student has a receptive mind

and wishes to make himself at one with nature, can he be taught how to meditate, or does he have to develop his own form?

A. Nature? How do you mean?

Q. If he wishes to study, can he accept other people's teaching, or can he develop them himself?

A. In fact it is necessary to receive oral instruction, oral teaching. Though he must learn to give before he can accept anything, he must learn to surrender. Second, he finds that the whole idea of learning stimulates his understanding. Also this avoids building up a great feeling of achievement, as though everything is "my own work"—the concept of the self-made man.

Q. Surely that is not sufficient reason for going to receive instruction from a teacher, just to avoid the feeling that otherwise everything is self-made. I mean, in the case of someone like Ramana Maharshi, who attained realization without an external teacher, surely he shouldn't go and find a guru just in case he might become big-headed?

A. No. But he is exceptional, that is the whole point. There is a way, it is possible. And basically no one can transmit or impart anything to anybody. One has to discover within oneself. So perhaps in certain cases people could do that. But building up on oneself is somehow similar to ego's character, isn't it? One is on rather dangerous ground. It could easily become ego's activity, because there is already the concept of "I" and then one wants to build up more on that side. I think—and this may sound simple, but it is really the whole thing—that one learns to surrender gradually, and that surrendering the ego is a very big subject. Also, the teacher acts as a kind of mirror, the teacher gives back one's own reflection. Then for the first time you are able to see how beautiful you are, or how ugly you are.

Perhaps I should mention here one or two small points about meditation, although we have already discussed the general background of the subject.

Generally, meditation instruction cannot be given in a class. There has to be a personal relationship between teacher and pupil. Also there are certain variations within each basic technique, such as awareness of breathing. But perhaps I should briefly mention the basic way of meditating, and then, if you want to go further, I am sure you could do so and receive further instruction from a meditation teacher.

As we have mentioned already, this meditation is not concerned with trying to develop concentration. Although many books on Buddhism speak of such practices as shamatha as being the development of concentration, I think this term is misleading in a way. One might get the idea that the practice of meditation could be put to commercial use, and that one would be able to concentrate on counting money or something like that. But meditation is not just for commercial uses; it is a different concept of concentration. You see, generally one cannot really concentrate. If one tries very hard to concentrate, then one needs the thought that is concentrating on the subject and also something which makes that accelerate further. Thus there are two processes involved and the second process is a kind of watchman, which makes sure that you are doing it properly. That part of it must be taken away, otherwise one ends up being more self-conscious and merely aware that one is concentrating, rather than actually being in a state of concentration. This becomes a vicious circle. Therefore one cannot develop concentration alone, without taking away the centralized watchfulness, the trying to be careful—which is ego. So the shamatha practice, the awareness of breathing, is not concerned with concentrating on the breathing.

The cross-legged posture is the one generally adopted in the East, and if one can sit in that position, it is preferable to do so. Then one can train oneself to sit down and meditate anywhere, even in the middle of a field, and one need not feel conscious of having a seat or of trying to find something to sit on. Also, the physical posture does have a certain importance. For instance, if one lies down, this might inspire one to sleep; if one stands, one might be inclined to walk. But for those who find it difficult to sit cross-legged, sitting on a chair is quite good, and, in fact, in Buddhist iconography the posture of sitting on a chair is known as the Maitreya asana, so it is quite acceptable. The important thing is to keep the back straight so that there is no strain on the breathing. And for the breathing itself it is not a matter of concentrating, as we have already said, but of trying to become one with the feeling of breath. At the beginning some effort is needed, but after practicing for a while the awareness is simply kept on the verge of the movement of breath; it just follows it quite naturally and one is not trying particularly to bind the mind to breathing. One tries to feel the breath—outbreathing, inbreathing, outbreathing, inbreathing—and it usually happens that the outbreathing is longer than the inbreathing, which helps one to become aware of space and the expansion of breathing outward.

It is also very important to avoid becoming solemn and to avoid the feeling that one is taking part in some special ritual. One should feel quite natural and spontaneous, and simply try to identify oneself with the breath. That is all there is to it, and there are no ideas or analyzing involved. Whenever thoughts arise, just observe them *as thoughts,* rather than as being a subject. What usually happens when we have thoughts is that we are not aware that they are thoughts at all. Supposing one is planning one's next holiday trip: one is so engrossed in the thoughts that it is almost as though one were already on the trip and one is not even aware that these are thoughts. Whereas, if one sees that this is merely thought creating such a picture, one begins to discover that it has a less real quality. One should not try to suppress thoughts in meditation, but one should just try to see the transitory nature, the translucent nature of thoughts. One should not become involved in them, nor reject them, but simply observe them and then come back to the awareness of breathing. The whole point is to cultivate the acceptance of everything, so one should not discriminate or become in-volved in any kind of struggle. That is the basic meditation technique, and it is quite simple and direct. There should be no deliberate effort, no attempt to control and no attempt to be peaceful. This is why breathing is used. It is easy to feel the breathing, and one has no need to be self-conscious or to try and do anything. The breathing is simply available and one should just feel that. That is the reason why technique is important to start with. This is the primary way of starting, but it generally continues and develops in its own way. One sometimes finds oneself doing it slightly differently from when one first started, quite spontaneously. This is not classified as an advanced technique or a beginner's technique. It simply grows and develops gradually.

WISDOM

Prajna. Wisdom. Perhaps the English word has a slightly different sense. But the word used in Tibetan, *sherab,* has a precise meaning: *she* means knowledge, knowing, and *rab* means ultimate—so primary or first knowledge, the higher knowledge. So sherab is not specific knowledge in any technical or educational sense of knowing the theology of Buddhism, or knowing how to do certain things, or knowing the metaphysical aspect of the teaching. Here knowledge means knowing the situation, *knowingness* rather than actual knowledge. It is knowledge without a self, without the self-centered consciousness that one is knowing—which is connected with ego. So this knowledge—prajna or sherab—is broad and far-seeing, though at the same time it is tremendously penetrating and

exact, and it comes into every aspect of
our life. It therefore plays a very important
part in our development, as does upaya,
method, which is the skillful means for
dealing with situations in the right way.
These two qualities, in fact, are sometimes
compared to the two wings of a bird.
Upaya is also described in the scriptures as
being like a hand, which is skillful, and
prajna as being axlike, because it is sharp
and penetrating. Without the ax it would
be impossible to cut wood: one would simply hurt one's hand. So one may have the
skillful means without being able to put it
into effect. But if there is also prajna,
which is like an eye, or like light, then one
is able to act properly and skillfully.
Otherwise the skillful means might become foolish, for only knowledge makes
one wise. In fact upaya by itself could
make the greatest of fools, because everything would still be based on ego. One
might see the situation up to a point and

be partially able to deal with it, but one would not see it with clarity and without being affected by past and future, and one would miss the immediate nowness of the situation.

But perhaps we should examine how to develop this knowingness, or sherab, before we go into any further details. Now, there are three methods which are necessary for the cultivation of sherab, and these are known in Tibetan as töpa, sampa, and gompa. Töpa means to study the subject, sampa means to contemplate it, and gompa means to meditate and develop samadhi through it. So first töpa — study — which is generally associated with technical knowledge and the understanding of the scriptures and so on. But true knowledge goes much further than that, as we have already seen. And the first requirement for töpa is to develop a kind of bravery, to become a great warrior. We have mentioned this concept before, but perhaps it would be as well to go into it in more detail. Now, when the true warrior goes into battle he does not concern himself with his past and with recollections of his former greatness and strength, nor is he concerned with the consequences for the future and with thoughts of victory or defeat, or pain and death. The greatest warrior knows himself and has great confidence in himself. He is simply conscious of his opponent. He is quite open and fully aware of the situation, without thinking in terms of good and bad. What makes him a great warrior is that he has no opinions; he is simply aware. Whereas his opponents, being emotionally involved in the situation, would not be able to face him, because he is acting truly and sailing through their fear and is able to attack the enemy with effect. Therefore töpa, study and understanding, demands the quality of a great warrior. One should try to develop theoretical knowledge without being concerned with the past or the future. At first one's theories may be inspired by reading books, so we do not altogether dismiss learning and studying, which are very important and can provide a source of inspiration. But books can also become merely a means to escape from reality; they can provide an excuse for not really making an effort to examine things in detail for oneself. Reading can be rather like eating food. Up to a point one eats from physical necessity, but beyond that one is doing it for pleasure, because one likes the taste of food, or possibly just to fill up time: it is either breakfast time or lunch time or tea time or time for dinner. In the development of sherab it is clear that we do not read merely to accumulate information. We should read with great openness without making judgments, and just try to receive. The analogy is sometimes made of a child in a toy shop. He is so interested in everything that he becomes one with all the toys in the shop, and finally he has great difficulty in deciding which one to buy. He loses the very concept of having an opinion, such as "I want to buy this, I don't want to buy that." He becomes one with everything to such a point that he just can't decide. Learning should be like that, without opinions ("I like this, I don't like that"), but just accepting—not because it is in the scriptures or because some teacher says so and you have to accept it as an authority, nor because you don't have the right to criticize—but rather accepting out of sheer openness, without any obstacles. So read and study and develop a kind of inspiration from it. You can get a great deal from all kinds of books, but there is a limit, and when you develop a kind of general inspiration and self-confidence, then you should stop reading.

This is the first stage of töpa, where one develops theory. And it often happens at a certain point that this theory appears almost in the guise of experience, so that one may feel one has reached a state of spiritual ecstasy or enlightenment. There is a great excitement and one almost feels one has seen Reality itself. One may even be so carried away as to start writing great essays on the subject. But at this stage one must be very careful and try to avoid laying too much emphasis on the belief that one has·made some wonderful new discovery. The exciting part of it should not be too important; the main thing is how to put your knowledge into effect; otherwise one becomes like a poor beggar who has just discovered a sack of gold. He is overcome with excitement at having found it because in his mind gold is vaguely associated with food. But he has no idea how to put it to use by buying and selling to actually obtain the food. He has never dealt with that side of it before, so it is rather a problem. Similarly, one should not be overexcited by one's discovery. One has to exercise some restraint, although this experience may be even more exciting than reaching the state of Buddhahood. The trouble is that one sets such a high value on this knowledge, and by being too excited about it one is prevented from going beyond the dualistic way of seeing the situation. One attaches a great deal of importance to one's achievement, with the result that this excitement is still based on the self, on ego. Therefore one has to deal with it skillfully and even apply sherab, wisdom, to cope with the situation. So what one has found has to be put into effect immediately. It must not become a kind of tool that one merely shows off to other people. Nor must one become addicted to it, but use it only when the need arises.

Of course this theoretical knowledge is very interesting. One can talk so much about it—there are a great many words involved—and there is great pleasure in telling other people all about it. One may spend hours and hours talking and arguing and trying to demonstrate one's theory and prove its validity. One even develops a kind of evangelical attitude of trying to convert others to one's discovery, because one is intoxicated by it.

But that is still theory. And from there we come to sampa, which is reflective meditation, or contemplating and pondering on the subject. Sampa is not meditating in the sense of developing mindfulness and so on, but meditating on the subject and digesting it properly. In other words what one has learned is not yet sufficiently developed to enable one to deal with the practical things of life. For example, one might be talking about one's great discovery when some catastrophe occurs; say, the milk boils over or something like that. It might be something quite ordinary, but it seems to be rather exciting and terrible in a way. And the transition, from discussing this subject to controlling the milk, is just too much. The one is so elevated and the other is so ordinary and mundane that somehow one finds it very difficult to put one's knowledge into effect on that level. The contrast is too great and, as a result, one become upset, suddenly switches off and returns to the ordinary level of ego. So in this kind of situation there is a big gap between the two things, and we have to learn to deal with this and somehow make the connection with everyday life, and to identify our activities with what we have learned in the way of wisdom and theoretical knowledge. Of course our theory is something far beyond just ordinary theory, which one might have worked out mathematically to produce a feasible proposition. One is involved and there is great feeling in it. Nevertheless this is only theory, and for that very reason one finds it difficult to put it into effect. It seems true, it seems to convey something, when you only think on that subject, but it tends to remain static.

So sampa, reflective meditation, is necessary because one needs to calm down after the initial excitement of discovery and one has to find a way of relating one's newfound knowledge to oneself on a practical level. Suppose, for example, that you are just sitting at home with your family around you, having a cup of tea. Everything is normal and you are quite comfortable and contented. Now, how are you to link your exciting discovery of transcendental knowledge with that particular situation, with the feeling of that particular moment? How can one apply sherab, wisdom, in that particular environment? Of course, one generally associates "wisdom" with some special activity and one immediately rejects the present situation. One tends to think, "Well, what I have been doing up to now is not the *real* thing, so what I must do is leave here and go to such-and-such a place. I must go and practice and digest my knowledge in the wilds of Scotland—in a Tibetan monastery." But something is not quite right, because sooner or later you have to return to that same familiar street and those same familiar people, and everyday life continues on and on; one can never escape from it. So the point is, one must not try to change the situation—in fact one cannot. Since you are not a king, who could just give an order and stop things happening, you can only deal with what is nearest to you, which is yourself. Still you have a certain amount of apparent freedom to make decisions, and you may decide to go away. But in reality that is another way of trying to stop the world, though of course everything depends on your attitude. If one is thinking only in terms of trying to learn something further and not of rejecting one's environment, that is fine. The difficulty arises because one tends to go away after a particular incident where things seemed rather unreal and unpleasant, and one has the idea that if only one were in a special environment, or situation, one would see it all clearly. But that is a way of putting things off until tomorrow, and that will not do at all. This doesn't mean, of course, that one should not go to a meditation center and study or go into retreat for a period, but it should not be trying to escape. Though one may be able to open oneself more in that particular place, that does not mean that the external situation alone could enable one to change and develop. One must not blame one's surroundings, one must not blame people, one must not blame external conditions, but without trying to change anything, just step in and try to observe. That is real sampa, real contemplation on the subject. And when one is able to overcome the romantic and emotional attitude, one discovers truth even in the kitchen sink. So the whole point is not to reject, but to make use of that very moment, whatever the situation may be, and accept it, and respect it.

If you can be as open as that, then you will learn something without fail—this can be guaranteed, not because I am such an authority to say so, but because it is a fact. This has been tested over thousands of years, it has been proved and practiced by all the great adepts of the past. It is not something which has been achieved only by Buddha himself, but there is a long tradition of examining, studying and testing by many great teachers, like the long process of purifying gold by beating and hammering and melting it down. Still, it is not enough to accept this on anyone's authority. One must go into it and see it for oneself. So the only thing to do is to put it into effect and start meditating on the subject of prajna, which is very important here, for prajna alone can deliver us from self-centeredness, from ego. Teachings without prajna would still bind us, as they would merely add to the world of samsara, the world of confusion. One may even practice meditation or read scriptures or attend ceremonies, but without prajna there would be no liberation, without prajna one would be unable to see the situation clearly. That is to say that without prajna one would start from the wrong point, one would start by thinking, "I would like to achieve such-and-such, and once I have learned, how happy I will be!" At this stage prajna is *critical insight,* which is the opposite of ignorance, of ignoring one's true nature. Ignorance is often represented symbolically as a pig, because the pig never turns his head but just snuffles on and on and eats whatever comes in front of him. So it is prajna which enables us not merely to consume whatever is put in front of us, but to see it with critical insight.

Finally we come to gompa, meditation. First we had theory, then contemplation, and now meditation in the sense of samadhi. The first stage of gompa is to ask oneself, "Who am I?" Though this is not really a question. In fact it is a statement, because "Who am I?" contains the answer. The thing is not to start from "I" and then want to achieve something, but to start directly with the subject. In other words one starts the real meditation without aiming for anything, without the thought, "I want to achieve." Since one does not know "Who am I?" one would not start from "I" at all, and one even begins to learn from beyond that point. What remains is simply to start on the subject, to start on what *is,* which is not really "I am." So one goes directly to that, directly to the "is." This may sound a bit vague and mysterious, because these terms have been used so much and by so many people; we must try then to clarify this by relating it to ourselves. The first point is not to think in terms of "I," "I want to achieve." Since there is no one to do the achieving, and we haven't even grasped that yet, we should not try to prepare anything at all for the future.

There is a story in Tibet about a thief who was a great fool. He stole a large sack of barley one day and was very pleased with himself. He hung it up over his bed, suspended from the ceiling, because he thought it would be safest there from the rats and other animals. But one rat was very cunning and found a way to get to it. Meanwhile the thief was thinking, "Now, I'll sell this barley to somebody, perhaps my next-door neighbor, and get some silver coins for it. Then I could buy something else and then sell that at a profit. If I go on like this I'll soon be very rich, then I can get married and have a proper home. After that I could have a son. Yes, I shall have a son! Now what name shall I give him?" At that moment the moon had just risen and he saw the moonlight shining in through the window onto his bed. So he thought, "Ah, I shall call him Dawa" (which is the Tibetan word for moon). And at that very moment the rat had finished eating right through the rope from which the bag was hanging, and the bag dropped on the thief and killed him.

Similarly, since we haven't got a son and we don't even know "Who am I?," we should not explore the details of such fantasies. We should not start off by expecting any kind of reward. There should be no striving and no trying to achieve anything. One might then feel, "Since there is no fixed purpose and there is nothing to attain, wouldn't it be rather boring? Isn't it rather like just being nowhere?" Well, that is the whole point. Generally we do things because we want to achieve something; we never do anything without first thinking, "Because . . ." "I'm going for a holiday *because* I want to relax, I want a rest." "I am going to do such-and-such *because* I think it would be interesting." So every action, every step we take, is conditioned by ego. It is conditioned by the illusory concept of "I," which has not even been questioned. Everything is built around that and everything begins with "because." So that is the whole point. Meditating without any purpose may sound boring, but the fact is we haven't sufficient courage to go into it and just give it a try. Somehow we have to be courageous. Since one is interested and one wants to go further, the best thing would be to do it perfectly and not start with too many subjects, but start with one subject and really go into it thoroughly. It may not sound interesting, it may not be exciting all the time, but excitement is not the only thing to be gained, and one must also develop patience. One must be willing to take a chance and in that sense make use of will power.

One has to go forward without fear of the unknown, and if one does go a little bit further, one finds it is possible to start without thinking "because," without thinking "I will achieve something," without just living in the future. One must not build fantasies around the future and just use that as one's impetus and source of encouragement, but one should try to get the real feeling of the present moment. That is to say that meditation can only be put into effect if it is not conditioned by any of our normal ways of dealing with situations. One must practice meditation directly without expectation or judgment and without thinking in terms of the future at all. Just leap into it. Jump into it without looking back. Just start on the technique without a second thought. Techniques, of course, vary a great deal, as everything depends on the person's character. Therefore no generalized technique can be suggested.

Well, those are the methods by which wisdom, sherab, can be developed. Now, wisdom sees so far and so deep, it sees before the past and after the future. In other words wisdom starts without making any mistakes, because it sees the situation so clearly. So for the first time we must begin to deal with situations without making the blind mistake of starting from "I" — which doesn't even exist. And having taken that first step, we will find deeper insight and make fresh discoveries, because for the first time we will see a kind of new dimension: we will see that one can in fact be at the end result at the same time that one is traveling along the path. This can only happen when there is no *I* to start with, when there is no expectation. The whole practice of meditation is based on this ground. And here you can see quite clearly that meditation is not trying to escape from life, it is not trying to reach a utopian state of mind, nor is it a question of mental gymnastics. Meditation· is just trying to see what *is,* and there is nothing mysterious about it. Therefore one has to simplify everything right down to the immediate present practice of what one is doing, without expectations, without judgments and without opinions. Nor should one have any concept of being involved in a battle against "evil" or of fighting on the side of "good." At the same time one should not think in terms of being limited, in the sense of not being allowed to have thoughts or even think of "I," because that would be confining oneself in such a small space that it would amount to an extreme form of sila, or discipline. Basically there are two stages in the practice of meditation. The first involves disciplining oneself to develop the first starting point of meditation, and here certain techniques, such as observing the breathing, are used. At the second stage one surpasses and sees the reality behind the technique of breathing, or whatever the technique may be, and one develops an approach to actual reality through the technique, a kind of feeling of becoming one with the present moment.

This may sound a little bit vague. But I think it is better to leave it that way, because as far as the details of meditation are concerned I don't think it helps to generalize. Since the techniques depend on the need of the person, they can only be discussed individually; one cannot conduct a class on meditation practice.